Living in Families

The Laidlaw Social Studies Series   **Skills and Concepts for Responsible Citizenship**

Beverly Jeanne Armento   **Jesus Garcia**   **Roy Erickson**

Herbert C. Rudman

Katherine T. Croft   Barbara Foney   Francie D. Johnson   Marilyn Walker

LAIDLAW BROTHERS • PUBLISHERS

A Division of Doubleday & Company, Inc.

RIVER FOREST, ILLINOIS

Sacramento, California   Chamblee, Georgia   Dallas, Texas   Toronto, Canada

The Laidlaw Social Studies Series   Skills and Concepts for Responsible Citizenship

Living With People   Living in Families

Living in Neighborhoods   Living in Communities   Living in World Regions

Living in Our Country   Living in the World

Acknowledgments

Project Director Wayne H. Talley / *Editors* Diane Gonciarz, Mary C. Ouska /
Production Director LaVergne G. Niequist / *Production Supervisor* Kathleen Kasper /
Production Staff Michaline V. Mankus / *Photo Researcher* William A. Cassin /
Art Director Gloria J. Muczynski / *Designer* Dennis Horan / *Artists* Frank Larocco;
Keith Neely; John Walter and Associates: Joanna Adamska-Koperska, Leon Bishop,
Dan Siculan, and Jack Wallen

Photo Credits

Camerique, cover, pages 1, 3-5.
Alpha/D. Ellefsen, 19 (right). Alpha/P. Gridley, 33. Alpha/Elyse Lewis, 50. Alpha/J. McNee, 51 (left). Alpha/R. Rowan, 18 (right). American Red Cross National Headquarters, Photo Section, 56. Artstreet, 78 (left), 111 (right), 112 (right), 120 (bottom), 121. Berg & Associates, 112 (left). The Bettmann Archive, 102. Jim Bradshaw, 13 (right), 47 (left). Cameramasters, 52 (right). Camerique, 15 (left), 86 (left), 109 (left). Click/Chicago Ltd./Philippe Achache, 129 (top right). Click/Chicago Ltd./David Reed, 129 (left). Harry Cohen, 77, 86 (right). Corn's Photo Service, 119 (right). Corn's Photo Service/Cindy Ann Corn, 89 (right). Betty Crowell, 130 (right).
Dr. E.R. Degginger, 25 (left), 54 (top). Leo de Wys Inc., 124 (left). Joseph A. Di Chello, Jr., 8 (left), 10 (left), 49 (left), 107 (top). Jacqueline Durand, 88 (left), 90 (right), 91 (right), 103 (right), 108 (right). Suzanne J. Engelmann, 133 (bottom right). S. Feldheim, 65 (both). FPG/Dennis Hallinan, 17 (left), 109 (right). FPG/Jim Howard, 58 (left). FPG/George Hunter, 19 (left). Grant Heilman, 104 (right), 105 (both), 107 (bottom), 111 (left). Historical Pictures Service, 94. Brent Jones, 13 (left), 15 (right), 17 (right), 21 (both), 49 (right), 57 (left), 88 (right), 91 (left). Kenji Kerins, 8 (right), 16 (left), 27, 44-45, 66 (left), 70, 80 (top), 84, 87 (right). Don Lansu, 10 (right), 46, 85 (both), 90 (left). Christopher Mankus, 9 (left), 11 (right), 12 (left), 22-23, 26, 29, 42, 53, 55 (all), 58 (right), 60, 61 (top), 63 (right), 64 (both), 68 (both), 72-73, 75, 76 (both), 79 (right), 80 (bottom), 81, 82 (both), 83 (both), 92. Norma Morrison, 48, 51 (right), 116-117, 133 (bottom left), 133 (top), 134, 135, 136. Odyssey Productions/Robert Frerck, 18 (left), 124 (right), 125. Joe Outland, 67. Connie and P.C. Peri, 6-7, 9 (right), 20, 54 (bottom), 59, 61 (bottom), 62, 87 (left), 106 (right), 120 (top). Photo Trends/Victoria Beller-Smith, 63 (left). Photo Trends/G. Granham, 129 (bottom right). Photo Trends/Jane Latta, 126. Photri, 24, 25 (top right), 30, 104 (left), 110 (right), 115. Photri/A. Novak, 78 (right). James H. Pickerell, 12 (right). Picture Group/Kevin Horan, 89 (left). Picture Group/James Pozarik, 95, 103 (left), 114. G.R. Roberts, 119 (left), 122 (right). Mick Roessler, 122 (left), 130 (left). Southern Light/Bohdan Hrynewych, 110 (left). Tom Stack & Associates/Don C. Arns, 66 (right). Taurus, 47 (right). Taurus/Mrs. T.W. Bennett, 128 (top). Taurus/Alec Duncan, 108 (left). Taurus/Kaz Mori, 25 (bottom right). Taurus/B.I. Ullmann, 74. Taurus/Lenore Weber, 52 (left). Mary Elenz Tranter, 11 (left), 14, 16 (right), 57 (right), 71, 79 (left), 106 (left). Worldwide Photo Specialty, 128 (bottom).

ISBN 0-8445-6301-3

CONTENTS

LIST OF MAPS

LIST OF CHARTS

LIST OF GRAPHS

LIST OF UNIT–END SKILLS: BUILDING YOUR SKILLS

UNIT 1
WHAT IS A FAMILY?

The people in this picture belong to a special group.
What are the people in this group doing?
When have you ever done anything like this?

1 WHAT MAKES A FAMILY?

You belong to a **family**.
A family is a special group of people.
They usually live in the same home.

Some families have two parents.
Some families have a mother but not a
   father.
Other families have a father but not a
   mother.
Families have different numbers of
   children.

CHECKING   How are families different?

MAIN

IDEAS

2 PEOPLE IN FAMILIES SHARE

People in families care for one another.
They do things for one another.
Parents and children share the place
  where they live.
They also share pets and other things.

People in families help one another.
They help to take care of their home.
They help one another learn.

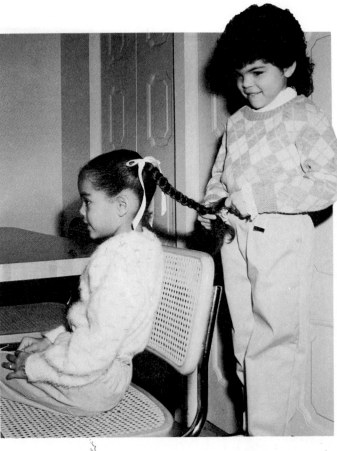

CHECKING

MAIN

IDEAS

1. How do people in families share with one another?

2. How do people in families help one another?

3 PEOPLE IN FAMILIES ACT TOGETHER

People in families do things together.
Sometimes they do things at home.
Many families like to play games.
Some families like to read.

Sometimes families do things away from home.
Some families like to visit friends.
Families also like to visit special places.
Some families like to go to the park.

CHECKING  What are some things people in families like to do together?

MAIN

IDEAS

Citizenship in Action

Big Brothers/Big Sisters of America

Big Brothers/Big Sisters is a group of grown-ups.

They help children who have only one parent.

Children do things with their Big Brother or Big Sister.

Big Brothers and Big Sisters are special friends.

4 FAMILIES CHANGE

Families **change,** or become different.
They change in many ways.
Some families become larger.
Other families become smaller.

The people in a family change.
Children grow bigger.
Everyone grows older.
Sometimes families change the place
where they live.

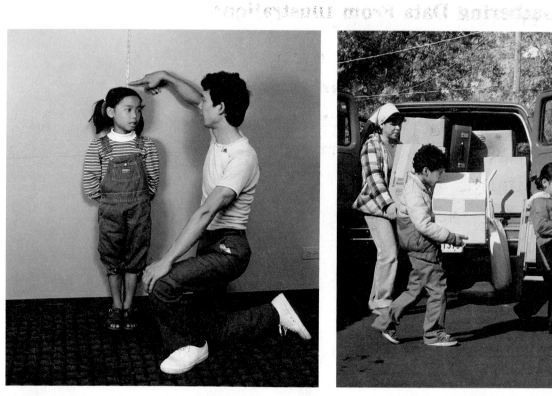

CHECKING In what ways do families change?

MAIN

IDEAS

Practicing Your Skills

Gathering Data From Illustrations

Pictures can help you learn.
They can help you learn about families.
Look at the pictures on this page.
How many people belong to each family?
What is each family doing?

5 FAMILIES ARE EVERYWHERE

People everywhere live in families.
Families are alike in certain ways.
People in families everywhere care for
  one another.
They do things together.

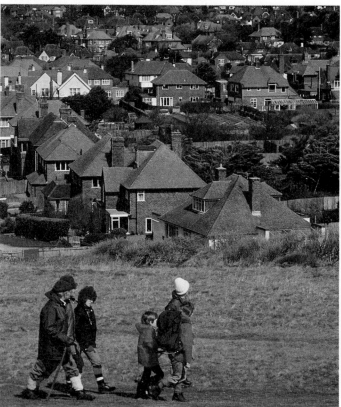

Families are also different in certain ways.
People in families may wear different clothes.
They may eat different foods.
Families live in different ways.

CHECKING MAIN IDEAS

1. How are families everywhere alike?

2. How are families everywhere different?

INVESTIGATING THE UNIT

Write your answers on a separate sheet of paper.

Using Words and Terms

Use the following words or terms in a sentence to show that you understand their meaning:

family   change

Understanding Ideas

1. In what ways are families different?
2. How do people in families care for one another?
3. How do families change?

Building Your Skills

Answer the questions about the pictures on this page.

1. Where is the family in each picture?
2. What is each family doing?
3. How many people are in the first picture?
4. How many people are in the second picture?

Making Decisions

You and a friend are playing.

Your younger brother wants to play.

What would you do?

Why would you do that?

UNIT 2
WHERE DO FAMILIES LIVE?

This family is planning a trip to the
zoo.
The children want to see the lions, the
monkeys, and the bears.
What is this family looking at?
How might it help the family know
where to go at the zoo?

22

1 ON THE EARTH

This is a picture of the earth.
It shows the earth from far away.
We live on the earth.

The earth has land.
Some of the land is hills or mountains.
Much of the land is flat.
The earth also has water.

CHECKING   Where do we live?

MAIN

IDEAS

Practicing Your Skills

Determining Relative Direction

Look at the picture of the family.

Mother is pointing down.

Father is pointing up.

Up and down are directions.

Directions help us find where things are.

Left and right are also directions.

Father is on the right.

What side is mother on?

2 WHAT GLOBES SHOW

This is a picture of a **globe.**
A globe is a model of the earth.
A globe shows places on the earth.

Directions help us find places on a
   globe.
North and south are directions.
East and west are also directions.
North is toward the North Pole.
South is toward the South Pole.
What direction is Carlos from Mary?

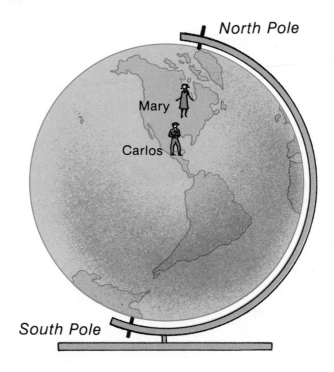

CHECKING MAIN IDEAS

1. What is a globe?
2. What do directions help us do?

3 WHAT MAPS SHOW

This is a picture.

What can you learn from the picture?

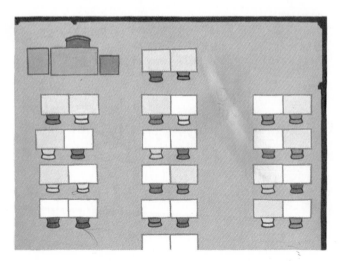

This is a **map** of the same place.

A map is a drawing of the earth.

A map shows all or part of the earth.

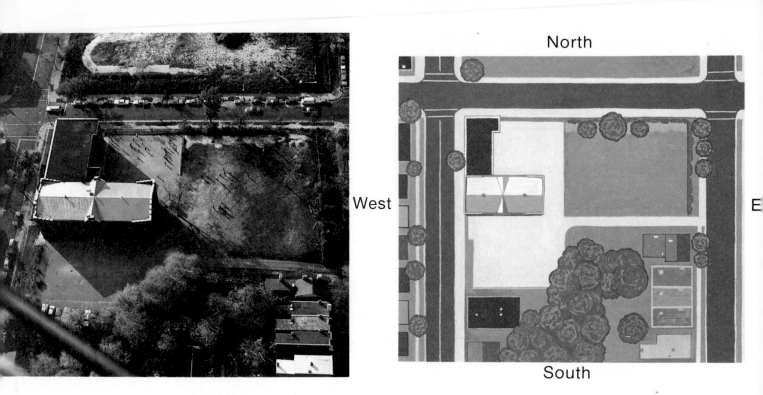

Directions are often written on a map.
What directions are written on this
  map?
Directions help us find places on a map.
What direction is the playground from
  the school?

CHECKING   What is a map?
MAIN
IDEAS

4 FINDING COUNTRIES

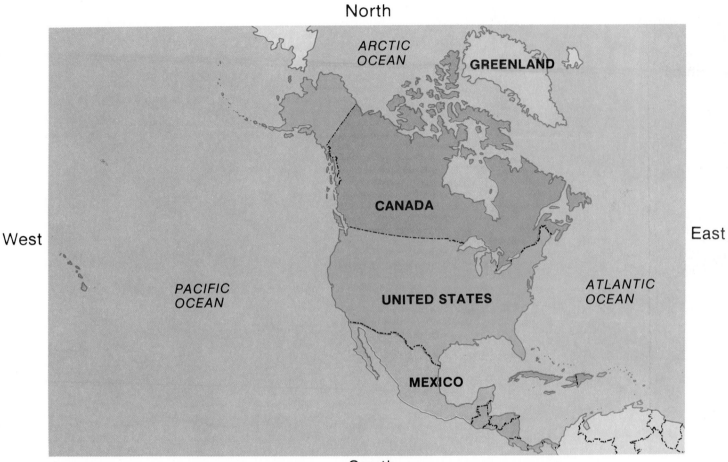

This map shows how people have
divided the earth into many parts.
These parts are called countries.
Some countries are large.
Other countries are small.

This map shows the United States.
It is the country we live in.

North

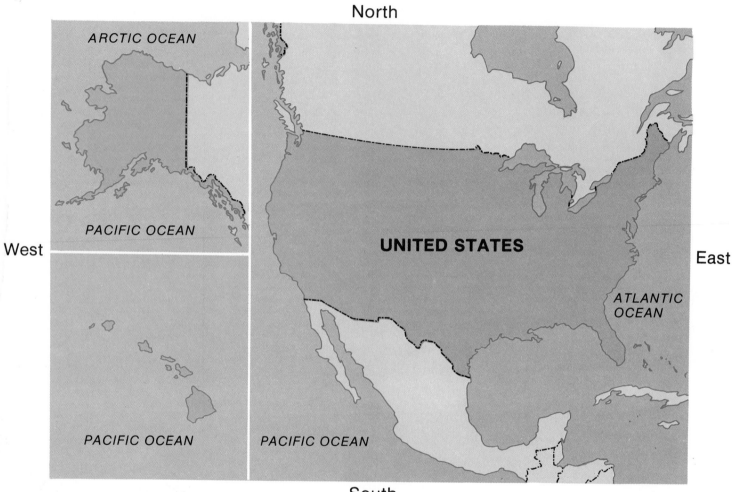

West

ARCTIC OCEAN

PACIFIC OCEAN

PACIFIC OCEAN

PACIFIC OCEAN

UNITED STATES

ATLANTIC
OCEAN

East

South

CHECKING What country do we live in?

MAIN

IDEAS

A Nation's Heritage

The White House

The White House is where the
President of our country lives and
works.
It is in Washington, D.C.
The President works on the first floor.
The President's family lives on the
second floor.

5 FINDING STATES

This map shows the United States.
People have divided the United States
   into many parts.
These parts are called states.

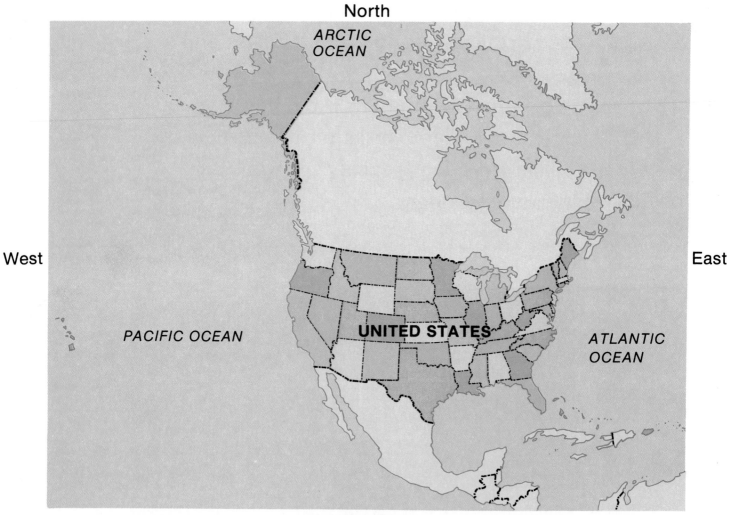

North

ARCTIC
OCEAN

West

East

PACIFIC OCEAN

UNITED STATES

ATLANTIC
OCEAN

South

Some states are large.
Other states are small.
Each state has a different name.

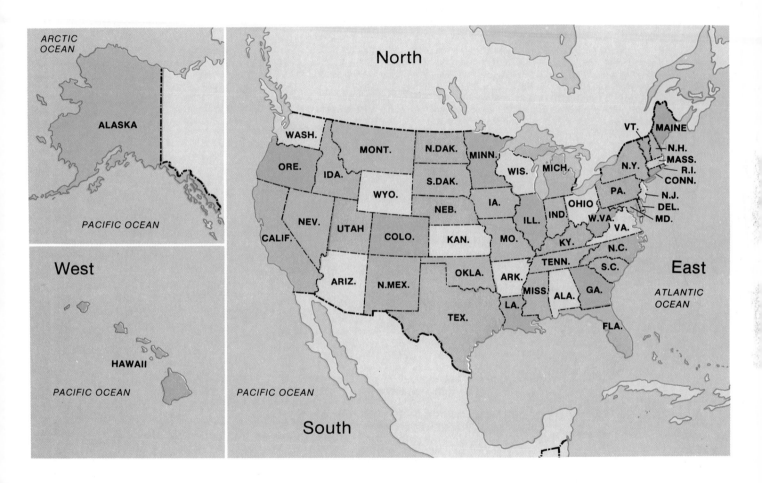

CHECKING

MAIN

IDEAS

What are the parts of the United States called?

6 FINDING WHERE WE ARE

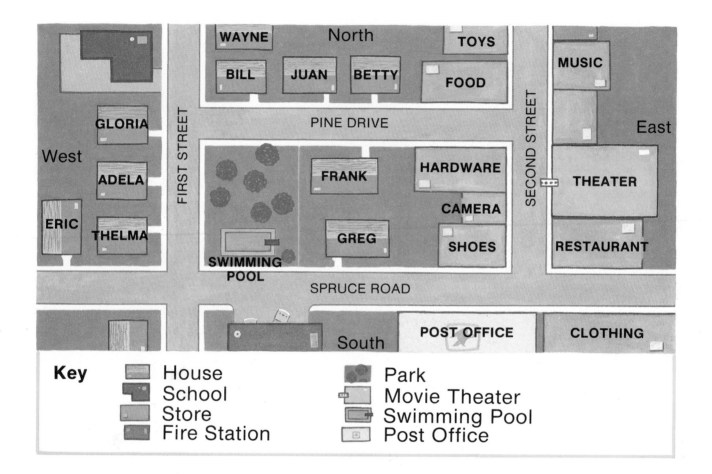

This is a map of a neighborhood.

This map uses **symbols** to show where things are.

A symbol is something that stands for something else.

A map usually has a **map key.**
The map key is a list of symbols used
on a map.
This key tells what each symbol stands
for.
What does a [ ] stand for?

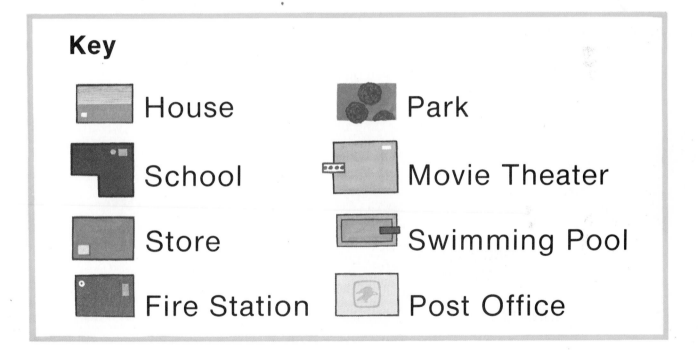

Key

House

Park

School

Movie Theater

Store

Swimming Pool

Fire Station

Post Office

CHECKING
MAIN
IDEAS

1. What is a symbol?
2. What tells you what map symbols stand for?

7 LOOKING AT CHARTS

This is a **chart.**
A chart shows facts in a way that is
easy to read.
This chart shows facts about what
families like to do.

Favorite Activities of Family Members

Activities	Carlos's Family	Mary's Family	Kari's Family	Jackie's Family
Watch Television	1	4	2	0
Read	3	1	4	2
Play Games	1	0	1	1
Swim	2	1	2	3

Look at this chart.

How many girls are there in Juan's family?

Whose family has the fewest boys?

Number of Children in Families

Families	Boys	Girls
Juan's Family	3	1
Karen's Family	1	2
Sasha's Family	0	3
Patrick's Family	2	2

CHECKING MAIN IDEAS   What does a chart show?

8 LOOKING AT GRAPHS

**Number of Family Members
Whose Favorite Activity Is Reading**

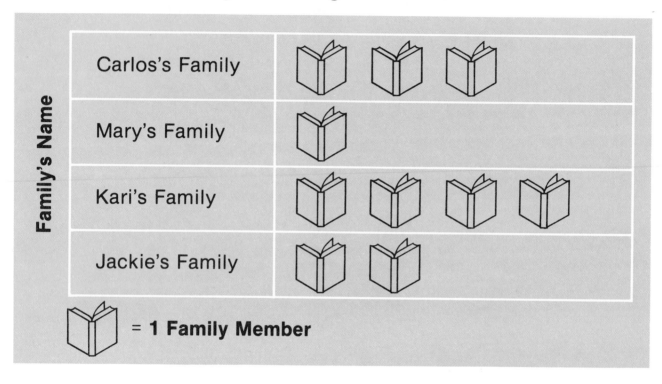

This is a **pictograph.**

A pictograph is a drawing.

It uses pictures to show numbers of
    things.

Each picture in this pictograph stands
    for one person.

**Number of Family Members
Whose Favorite Activity Is Reading**

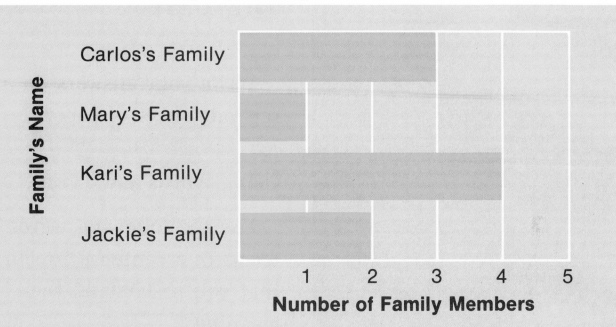

This is a **bar graph.**

A bar graph is a drawing.

It uses bars to show numbers of things.

How many people in Mary's family like
  to read?

CHECKING

MAIN

IDEAS

1. What is a pictograph?
2. What is a bar graph?

INVESTIGATING THE UNIT

Write your answers on a separate sheet of paper.

Using Words and Terms

Use the following words or terms in a sentence to show that you understand their meaning:

globe   chart   pictograph
map   map key   bar graph
symbols

Understanding Ideas

1. Where do we live?
2. What country do we live in?
3. What do we call the parts of the United States?

Building Your Skills

Answer the questions about the map.

1. What direction is Don's desk from Laura's desk?

2. Whose desk is west of Martha's desk?

3. What direction are the coat hooks from Jean's desk?

4. Whose desk is south of Jack's desk?

Making Decisions

Pretend that your family is planning to drive to another part of your state.

How might your family decide what roads to take and what to see?

What might your family use to plan its trip?

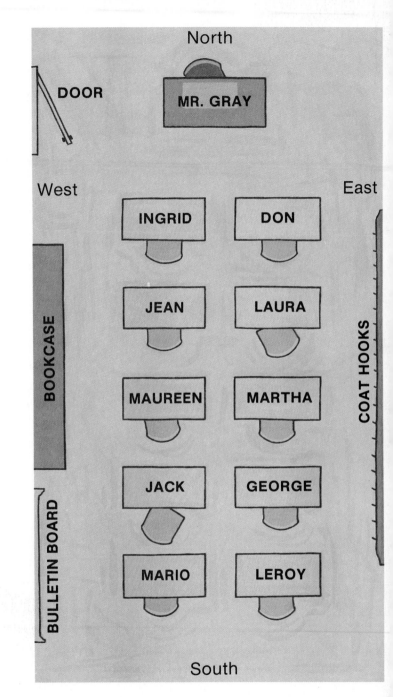

UNIT 3
FAMILY NEEDS AND WANTS

This family wants a pet.
How will the family get a pet?
What will the pet need?
What else might the family want?

1 WHAT NEEDS ARE

People live in families to fill their
  needs.
Needs are things people must fill in
  order to live.
Families need food, clothes, and a place
  to live.

Families need air and water.
They also need sleep.
People in families cannot do everything
 for themselves.
So they need other people.

CHECKING
MAIN
IDEAS

1. What are needs?
2. What are some needs families must fill?

2 FILLING THE NEED FOR FOOD

All people need food.
They need food in order to live.
Food helps people work and play.
Food helps people grow.
It helps people be healthy.

Families fill their need for food in
   different ways.
Some families grow food.
Some families buy food at markets.
Many families buy food in stores.

CHECKING
MAIN
IDEAS

1. Why do people need food?
2. How do families fill their need for
food?

3 FILLING THE NEED FOR CLOTHING

People need clothes.
Clothes protect people from the
  weather.
Some clothes are for warm weather.
Some clothes are for cold weather.
What clothes are for rain?

People sometimes wear special clothes.
Some clothes are for work.

Some clothes are for play.
What clothes would you wear to a
    party?

Families fill their need for clothes in different ways.
Some families make their own clothes.
Many families buy their clothes in stores.

CHECKING MAIN IDEAS

1. Why do people need clothes?
2. How do families fill their need for clothes?

4 FILLING THE NEED FOR HOUSING

People need **housing.**

Housing is a place to live.

People can eat and sleep in their housing.

They can be with their family.

Housing protects people from the weather.

Families live in many kinds of housing.
Some families live in houses.
Some families live in **mobile homes.**
Mobile homes are small houses that can
    be moved.

Many families live in **apartments.**
An apartment is a room or a group of
 rooms to live in.
There are two or more apartments in a
 building.

CHECKING
MAIN
IDEAS

1. Why do people need housing?
2. What kinds of housing do families
live in?

Citizenship in Action

The American Red Cross

People in the American Red Cross help
   families.
Sometimes water, wind, or fire destroys
   a family's home.
The American Red Cross helps the
   family.
It gives the family food and clothes.
It finds a place for the family to live.

5 WHAT WANTS ARE

Families have many **wants.**
Wants are things people wish to have.
People can live without these things.

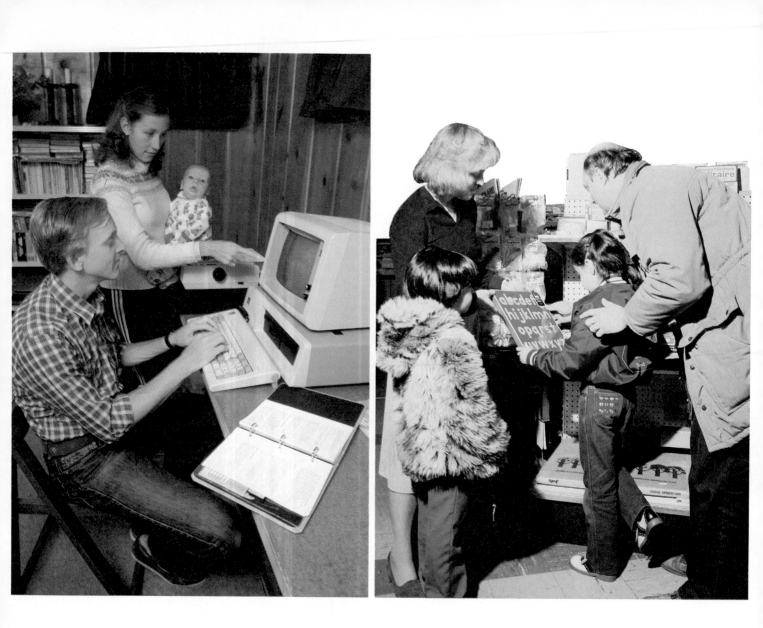

Different families have different wants.
Many families want a pet.
Some families want video games.
What do the families in the pictures
     want?

Families cannot have everything they
  want.
They must decide what wants to fill.
Families fill the wants that are
  important to them.

CHECKING   What are wants?

MAIN

IDEAS

6 BUYING GOODS

Families use many **goods.**

Goods are things.

Families use goods to fill needs and
wants.

Bread, houses, and shoes are goods.
These goods help families fill needs.
Radios and games are also goods.
These goods help families fill wants.

Some families make the goods they use.
Many families buy goods that other
    people have made.

CHECKING   1. What are goods?

MAIN   2. What do families use goods for?

IDEAS

7 BUYING SERVICES

Families use many **services.**
Services are jobs that people do for
others.
Doctors, teachers, and many other
people offer services.

Some services help fill needs.
A salesperson helps families fill the
    need for clothes.
Some services help fill wants.
What want is the person in the second
    picture helping a family fill?

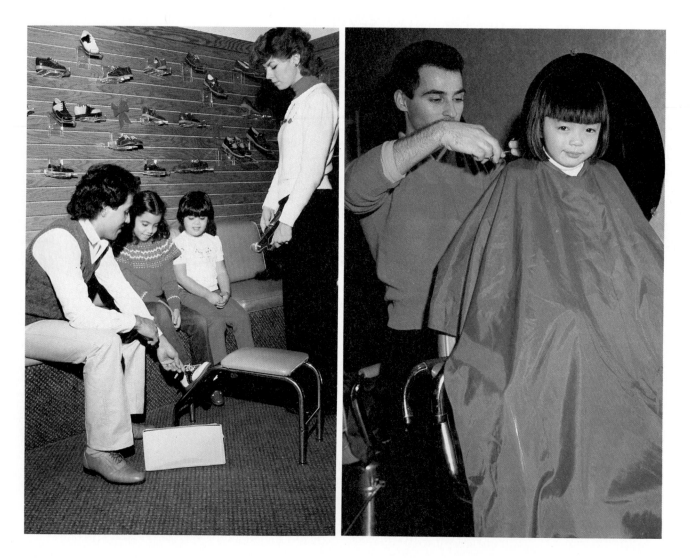

Families cannot do everything for
themselves.
They need other people to do things for
them.
Families pay for the services they use.

CHECKING

MAIN

IDEAS

1. What are services?
2. What do families use services for?

8 JOBS

People in families work.
They work to fill their family's needs.
They work to fill their family's wants.

People in families do different jobs.
Some people grow food.
Other people make goods.
Some people offer services.

People earn money for the jobs they do.
They use money to buy goods and
    services.
Families use these goods and services
    to fill their needs and wants.

CHECKING   Why do people in families work?

MAIN

IDEAS

Practicing Your Skills

Reading for General Information

You read to learn about many things.
Read the following to learn about
families:

Some families have two parents.
Some families have only a mother.
Other families have only a father.
Families have different numbers of
children.

What did you learn about families?

INVESTIGATING THE UNIT

Write your answers on a separate sheet of paper.

Using Words and Terms

Use the following words or terms in a sentence to show that you understand their meaning:

needs	goods
wants	services

Understanding Ideas

1. What needs do families have?

2. Why must families decide what wants to fill?

3. What do people buy with the money they earn?

Building Your Skills

Look at the picture and the maps at the right.

1. Which map shows the room in the picture?

2. What things are both in the picture and on the map?

3. What things are in the picture but not on the map?

Making Decisions

You want two different games.

You can play one game alone.

You need other people to play the other game.

You can buy only one game.

Which game would you buy?

How would you decide which game to buy?

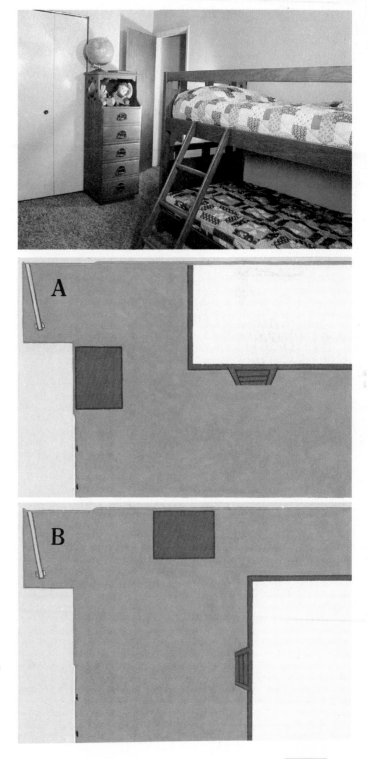

UNIT 4
ROLES AND RULES IN FAMILIES

Families do many things together.
What is the family in this picture
   doing?
What things do you do with your
   family?

1 LEARNING

You learn many things from your
   family.
Your family teaches you how to do new
   things.
Your family tells you about many things
   that you do not know.

You learn how to get along with people
in your family.
Your family also teaches you how to get
along with other people.
Young children can teach other people
in a family.
You can teach your family things, too.

CHECKING

MAIN

IDEAS

What kinds of things can you learn
from your family?

2 SHARING

People in families share many things
with one another.
Parents share their home.
Sisters and brothers sometimes share
their toys.
Other people in families share things
they own.

All people in families share their
feelings.
Love is a feeling people share.
They share happiness.
They share other feelings, too.

**CHECKING
MAIN
IDEAS**

What things do family members share
with one another?

A Nation's Heritage

Walt Disney World in Florida

Families sometimes take trips.
Many families visit Walt Disney World.
It is a good place for family fun.
Families also learn about our country's
past at Walt Disney World.

3 WORKING

A family has much work to do.
Some people must clean the house.

Some people must buy and cook food.
In some families young children must
be cared for.

People in families often share work.
Grown-ups do many things.
Children do other things.

Some people in families decide who
should do certain things.
All the people in families help to do the
work.

**CHECKING
MAIN
IDEAS**

1. What kinds of work do people in families do?

2. How do family members decide what work to do?

4 FAMILY PROBLEMS

Families sometimes have problems.
A family may have problems when the
family changes.
Families may have problems when
people in families must do new
things.

 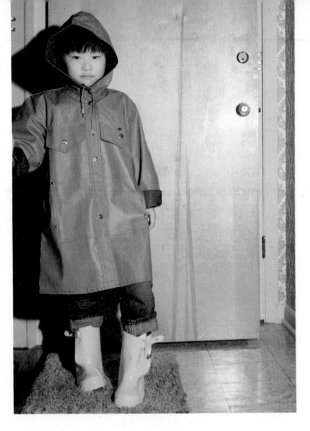

Rules can help people in families from
    having many problems.
Rules tell people how to act.
Rules tell people what to do.
Rules also tell people what not to do.

CHECKING

MAIN

IDEAS

1. When might families have
problems?

2. How can rules help families?

5 SOLVING PROBLEMS

People in families try to **solve** their
   problems.
People solve problems by finding
   answers to their problems.

Rules can help to solve problems.
Rules can help to keep the same
problems from happening again.
People in families can keep from having
some problems by following rules.

Sometimes people in families can solve
their own problems.
Sometimes people need the help of
someone else to solve their problems.

CHECKING
MAIN
IDEAS

1. How can rules help to solve problems?

2. What are some ways that people in families solve problems?

6 CHOOSING

Families must **choose** how to fill their
    needs and wants.
Families choose by picking what is
    important to them.
Families choose where to live.
They choose what to buy.
Families choose how to have fun.
They choose many other things.

Parents often choose what to buy
or to do.
Other people in families sometimes
choose, too.
Families choose what they need or want
most.
They choose what is important to them.

CHECKING MAIN IDEAS

1. How do families choose?
2. What are some things that families choose?

Citizenship in Action

Voting

People choose their country's leaders.
They choose by voting.
People vote for the President.
They also vote for people who make laws.
People vote for leaders of their
community.
Voting is very important.

7 PLANNING

Families **plan** how to fill their needs
    and wants.
Families plan by choosing what to do
    and what to buy.
They plan what to do today.
They also plan what to do tomorrow.

Families plan for things that will
    happen at a much later time.
They may plan to buy a home or a car.
They may plan a trip.
These things may cost a lot of money.
So families must save money for these
    things.

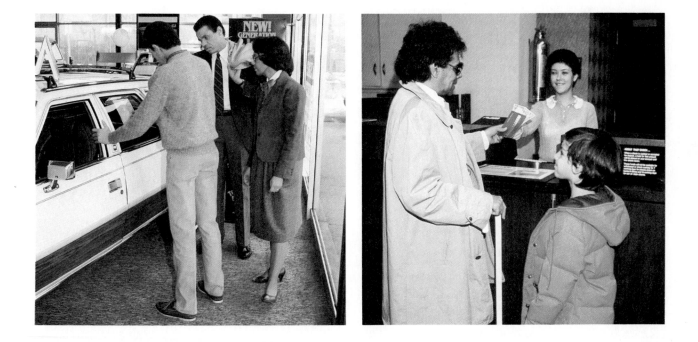

CHECKING MAIN IDEAS

1. What do families do when they plan?

2. Why do families save money?

INVESTIGATING THE UNIT

Write your answers on a separate sheet of paper.

Using Words and Terms

Use the following words or terms in a sentence to show that you understand their meaning:

solve   choose   plan

Understanding Ideas

1. What things can family members teach one another?

2. What things can family members share with one another?

3. How do rules help families?

Building Your Skills

Answer the questions about the chart on this page.

1. How many people are in this family?
2. What is the name of each person in this family?
3. How many jobs need to be done?
4. What is the name of each job that needs to be done?
5. What jobs should each person do?

Making Decisions

Suppose a family member and you are having a problem.

You cannot solve the problem by yourself.

What would you do? Why?

Family Jobs

	Dad	Mom	Yoko	Jiro
Wash Dishes	X			
Dry Dishes		X		
Dust				X
Set Table				X
Polish Furniture	X			
Vacuum		X		
Take Out Garbage			X	

UNIT 5
FAMILIES
THEN AND NOW

Families have changed over the years.
Which family might you see today?
Which family might have lived a long
time ago?

6

- Canned Meat & Fish
- Coffee Filters
- Gourmet Foods
- Goya
- Italian Foods

- Kosher Foods
- Melba Toast
- Mexican Foods
- Oriental Foods
- Spanish Foods

PIECE OR...
DELI-SLICED
PASTRAMI
$129
½ LB

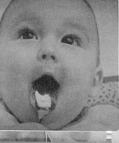

5

- Bakeware
- Bread Crumbs
- Cake Mixes
- Desserts
- Dietetic

1 THE FIRST AMERICAN FAMILIES

The first American families were
American Indians.
These people are sometimes called
native Americans.
They got their food in many ways.

American Indians picked wild fruits and
  nuts.
Some of these people hunted.
They hunted deer and buffalo.
Others fished.
Some American Indians grew food.
They grew corn and beans.

American Indians made their clothes.
Some American Indians used animal
hides.
Some used tree bark.

Native Americans made their houses.
They used wood, hides, and other
things.
Large houses with rounded roofs were
called **longhouses.**
Pointed houses were called **tepees.**
Some American Indians made other
kinds of houses.

CHECKING MAIN IDEAS

1. Who were the first American families?

2. What were some of the ways that American Indians filled their needs?

2 PIONEER FAMILIES

Some people who moved west long ago
   were called **pioneers.**
They moved to parts of the United
   States where few people lived.
Pioneer families often made houses of
   logs.
These houses were called **log cabins.**

Pioneer families usually lived on farms.
They grew much of their food.
They also hunted for food.
Pioneer families made most of their
   own clothes.
Pioneers often used animal hides to
   make their clothes.

CHECKING MAIN IDEAS

1. Who were pioneers?

2. How did pioneers get houses, food, and clothing?

A Nation's Heritage

Wagon Trains

Pioneer families moved west in covered
  wagons.
Many covered wagons moving together
  made up a **wagon train.**
The trip west was long and hard.
The pioneers stopped every night.
They cooked, slept, and rested the
  animals.

3 AMERICAN FAMILIES TODAY

Most people who live in the United
   States today were born here.
Many people also come from other
   countries to live in our country.
People come here to find jobs.
They come for other reasons, too.

Today families go to stores to buy most
of the things they need.
Families buy goods.
They buy food and clothes.
Families also buy services.
They buy the services of doctors and
many other people.

**CHECKING
MAIN
IDEAS**

1. Why do people come to the
United States from other countries?

2. How do families today get what
they need?

4 FAMILIES ON FARMS

Some families live on farms.
Some farmers grow crops.
Other farmers raise animals.
There is much work to do on a farm.
All the people in the family help.
Other people sometimes help, too.
Farmers also use machines to help
   them.

Farm families often use some of the
food from the farm.
Farm families buy things they need and
want from stores in nearby towns.
They buy both goods and services.
They buy farm machines and other
things.

**CHECKING
MAIN
IDEAS**

1. Who does the work on a farm?
2. How do farm families fill their
needs and wants?

5 FAMILIES IN TOWNS

Some families live in towns.
People in towns often live in houses
    that are not very close together.
Families in towns usually have only a
    few places to buy goods and services.

The stores in towns are often small.
Families buy some goods and services
in these stores.
They buy food, clothes, and many other
things.
Town families sometimes go to cities to
buy certain things.

CHECKING
MAIN
IDEAS

1. Where do people in towns often
live?

2. How do families in towns fill their
needs and wants?

6 FAMILIES IN CITIES

Many families live in cities.
Cities have many people.
So people often live close together.
Some families live in houses.
Other families live in apartments.
Some apartment buildings are very
   large and tall.

People in a city often shop **downtown.**
This is a part of a city with many
   stores.
There are also stores in other parts of a
   city.
Families have many places to buy goods
   and services.

CHECKING MAIN IDEAS

1. Why do people in cities often live close together?

2. Where do people in cities fill their needs and wants?

7 FAMILIES IN SUBURBS

Many families live in **suburbs.**
Suburbs are places near large cities.
Families in suburbs often live in
   houses.
Some families live in apartments.
Houses are often farther apart than in
   cities.

Families in suburbs often shop at
shopping centers.
These are places with many stores.
Families have many places to buy goods
and services.
Families in suburbs sometimes go to
the city to shop and do other things.

CHECKING
MAIN
IDEAS

1. What are suburbs?

2. Where do families in suburbs fill
their needs and wants?

Practicing Your Skills

Comparing Data

Maps can help you learn.
Use the map key to help you answer
   the questions.

Which place has more houses?
Which place has more space between
   buildings?
Which place has more trees?

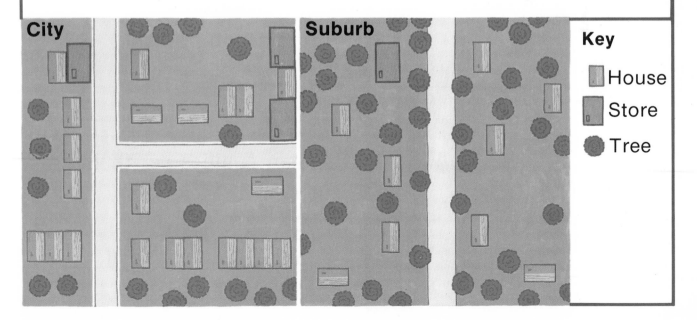

City

Suburb

Key

House
Store
Tree

INVESTIGATING THE UNIT

Write your answers on a separate sheet of paper.

Using Words and Terms

Use the following words or terms in a sentence to show that you understand their meaning:

> native Americans
> pioneers
> suburbs

Understanding Ideas

1. How did American Indian families get their food, clothes, and houses?
2. How did pioneer families get their food, clothes, and houses?

3. How do families in towns, cities, and suburbs today get their food and clothes?

4. What kinds of places do families in towns, cities, and suburbs live in?

Building Your Skills

Answer the questions about the picture on this page.

1. Is this a picture of a farm, a town, a city, or a suburb?

2. How can you tell what kind of place the picture shows?

Making Decisions

Would you rather visit a farm, a town, a city, or a suburb? Why?

UNIT 6
FAMILIES
THROUGHOUT
THE WORLD

Families throughout the world are like
  one another in many ways.
They are also different.
How is the family in this picture like
  families in the United States?
How is it different?

1 FAMILIES TO THE NORTH (CANADA)

Brian lives in the country of Canada
  [KAN-uhd-uh].
He lives on a large farm.
Brian's parents own the farm.
They grow wheat and oats.

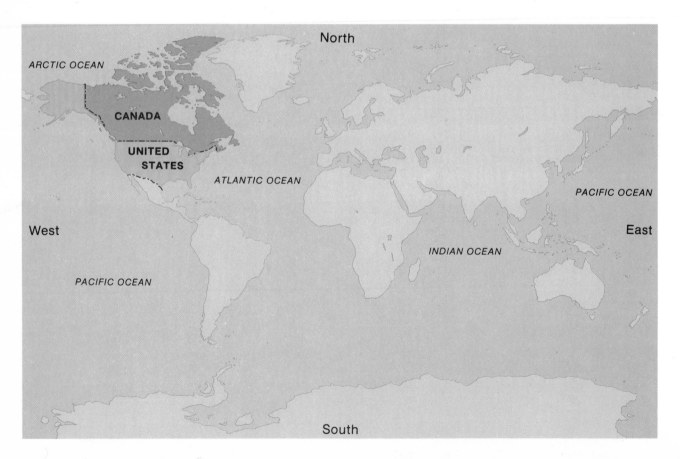

The people in Brian's family work
  together on the farm.
The older children work in the fields.
The younger children help in the
  garden.
They also help around the house.

Brian's family has needs.

The family raises some of the food it needs.

The family also buys food.

The people in Brian's family buy most of the clothes they wear.

The family lives in a house on the farm.

Brian and his family sell goods from
their farm to make money.
This money is used to fill needs.
It is also used to fill wants.
Brian and his family buy things they
need and want in a nearby town.

CHECKING MAIN IDEAS

1. How does Brian's family fill its needs?

2. How does Brian's family fill its wants?

A Nation's Heritage

Totem Poles

Some Indians in Canada use **totem poles** to tell about their family.

Totem poles are long poles made of wood.

Pictures of animals and people are cut into the wood.

Each picture on a totem pole stands for a person or for something that happened.

Totem poles help people remember what their family did in the past.

2 FAMILIES TO THE SOUTH (MEXICO)

Flora [FLOH-ruh] lives in the country
    of Mexico [MEK-si-KOH].
She and her family live in a small town.
Flora's father has a shop in town.
He makes and sells baskets.

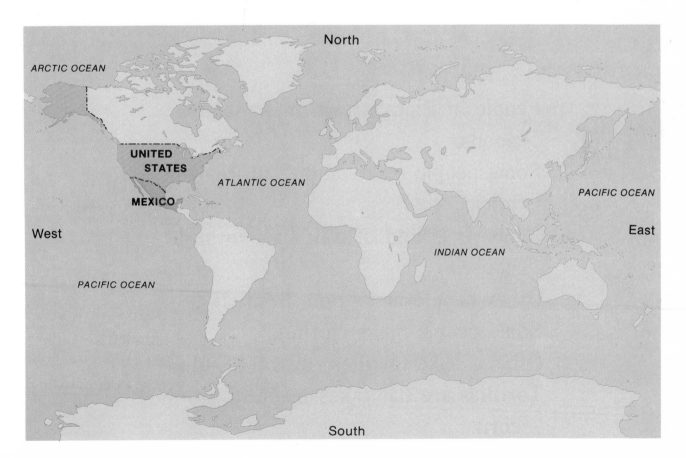

People in Flora's town make many
goods.
Some people make **adobe** [uh-DOH-bee]
bricks.
Adobe is a kind of clay used to build
houses.
Other people make pots from clay.
Some people make clothes.
Others make **tortillas** [tawr-TEE-uhz].
Tortillas are flat cakes made of ground
corn.

Some people in Flora's town offer
  services.
Teachers help children learn.
Barbers cut people's hair.
Some people repair things for others.

Some families in Flora's town earn
    money by making goods.
These families earn money by selling
    their goods in the market.
Other families in Flora's town earn
    money by offering services.
These families are paid for the services
    they do for others.

CHECKING
MAIN
IDEAS

1. What goods are made in Flora's town?

2. What services are offered in Flora's town?

3 FAMILIES ACROSS THE OCEAN (ENGLAND)

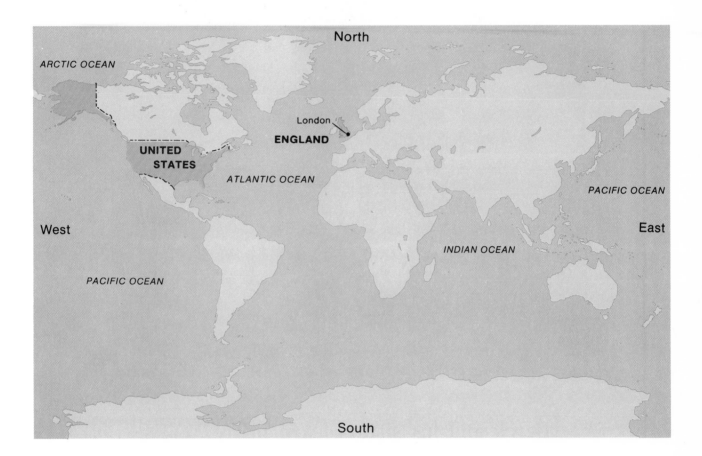

Derek [DER-ik] lives in the country of England [ING-gluhnd].
He and his family live in Barking.
Barking is a suburb of London [LUHN-duhn].

Derek and his sisters learn many
  things.
They learn at home from their parents.
They also learn in school.
Derek and his sisters walk to school.
Their school is for children of ages
  from five to eleven.

Derek's parents earn money for the
family.
His father makes automobiles.
Derek's mother is a nurse in London.
Derek and his sisters help around the
house.
They also help in the garden.

Derek and his family share.
They share a home.
They also share food.
Derek and his family have fun together.
Sometimes they go to the ocean to
   swim.
Sometimes they go horse riding.

CHECKING
MAIN
IDEAS

1. Where does Derek learn?
2. What are some things that Derek and his family do together?

130

Practicing Your Skills

Locating Suburbs and Towns Near London

This map shows some suburbs and
   towns near London.
Look at the map.
Answer the following questions:

What direction is Staines from London?
Which suburb is closer to London,
   Gerrards Cross or Denham?

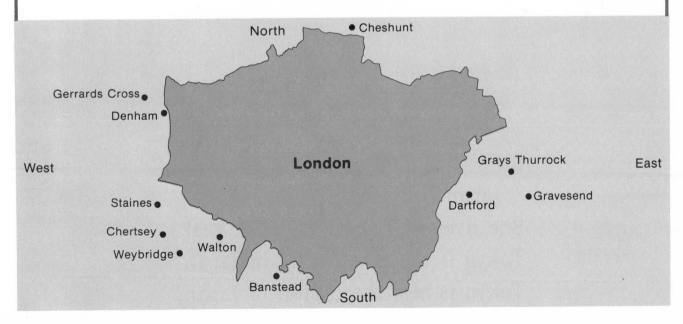

4 FAMILIES ACROSS THE OCEAN (JAPAN)

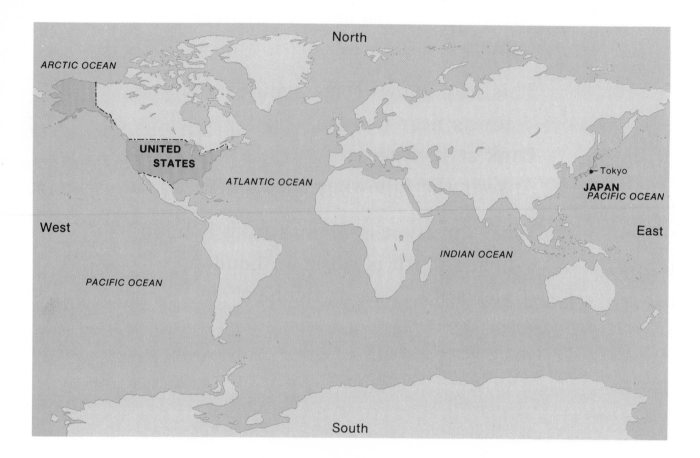

Kiku [KI-ku] lives in the country of
    Japan [juh-PAN].
She lives in Tokyo [TOH-kee-OH].
Tokyo is the largest city in Japan.
Tokyo is also the capital of Japan.

Kiku and her brothers go to school.
Kiku's parents earn money for the
   family.
After work, Kiku's mother takes care of
   the home.
Kiku also helps take care of the home.

Sometimes after work, Kiku's father
    visits with friends.
Kiku's father also helps with the work
    at home.
Sometimes he takes Kiku and her
    brothers to a park or a playground.

Kiku and her brothers have many rules
  to follow.
They must take off their shoes before
  entering their home.
They must obey their parents.
Kiku and her brothers must work hard
  in school.

CHECKING
MAIN
IDEAS

1. What does Kiku do for her family?

2. What are some rules Kiku has to
follow?

INVESTIGATING THE UNIT

Write your answers on a separate sheet of paper.

Using Words and Terms

Use the following words or terms in a sentence to show that you understand their meaning:

adobe
tortillas

Understanding Ideas

1. How do farm families in Canada fill their needs and wants?

2. How do families in towns in Mexico earn money?

3. What are some things people in families in England do together?

4. What are some rules that children in Japan follow?

Building Your Skills

Answer the questions about the pictograph below.

1. Whose family has the most people?

2. How many people are in Derek's family?

3. Whose family has the fewest people?

Making Decisions

Which of the countries you studied would you like to visit?

Why did you choose the country you chose?

Number of People in Each Family

Families		
Brian's	☺ ☺ ☺ ☺ ☺ ☺ ☺	
Flora's	☺ ☺ ☺	
Derek's	☺ ☺ ☺ ☺ ☺	
Kiku's	☺ ☺ ☺ ☺ ☺	

☺ = **1 person**

Handbook

The United States

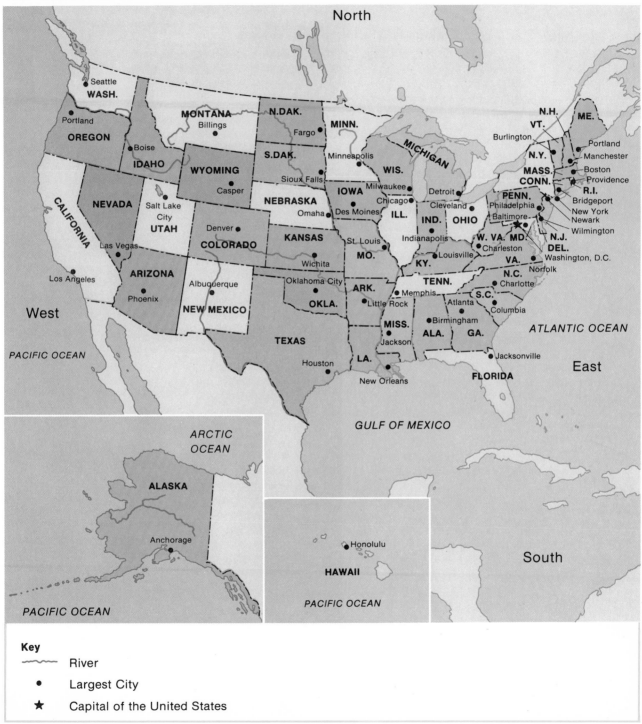

Key

~~~ River

• Largest City

★ Capital of the United States

139

The World

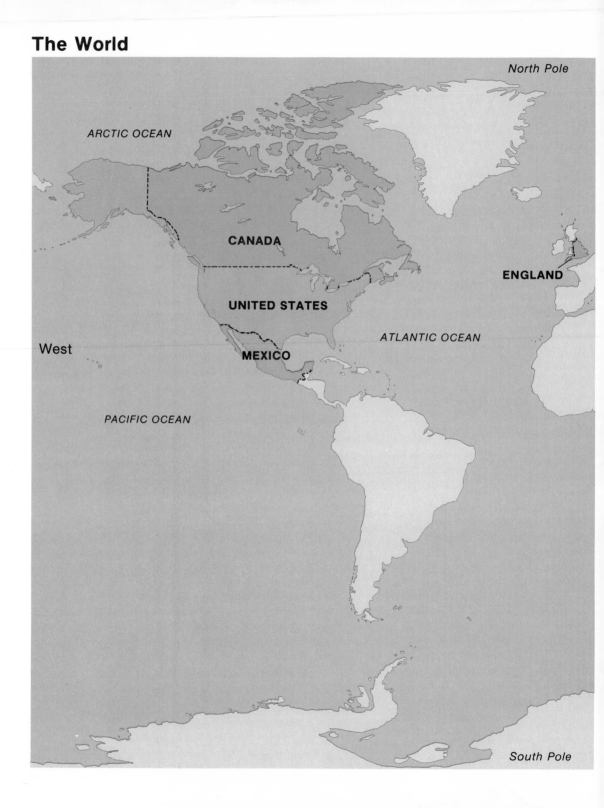

North Pole

ARCTIC OCEAN

CANADA

ENGLAND

UNITED STATES

West

MEXICO

ATLANTIC OCEAN

PACIFIC OCEAN

South Pole

North

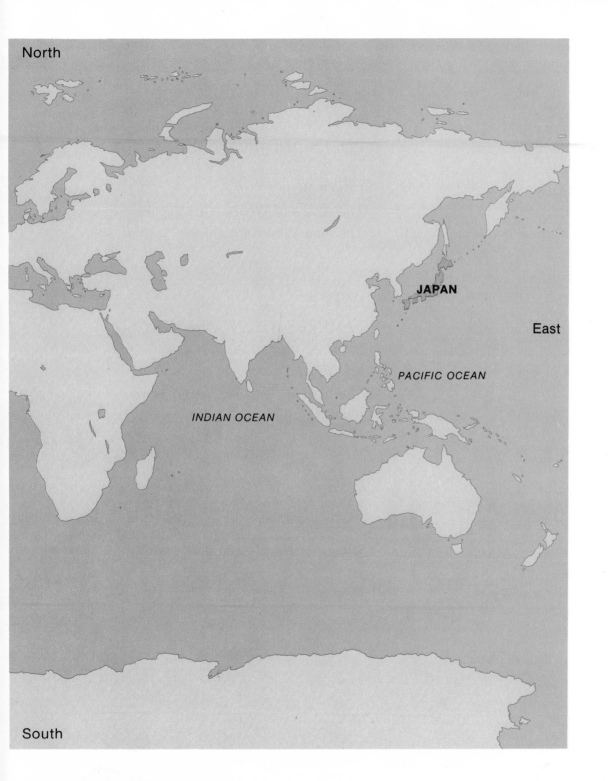

JAPAN

East

PACIFIC OCEAN

INDIAN OCEAN

South

BOOKS TO READ

UNIT 1

WHAT IS A FAMILY?

Your Family, My Family
The Hollywell Family
Breakfast With My Father

UNIT 2

WHERE DO FAMILIES LIVE?

The Discovery Book of Up & Down
Making Maps
Symbols and Their Meaning

UNIT 3

FAMILY NEEDS AND WANTS

From Cotton to Pants
When We Grow Up
An Apartment House Close Up

UNIT 4

ROLES AND RULES IN FAMILIES

I Can't Wait
The ABC's of What a Girl Can Be
The Man Who Kept House

UNIT 5

FAMILIES THEN AND NOW

The Pioneers
This Is How We Live in the Town
Indians

UNIT 6

FAMILIES THROUGHOUT THE WORLD

Take a Trip to England
Japan
Mexico

142

GLOSSARY

change

globe

choose

goods

family

map

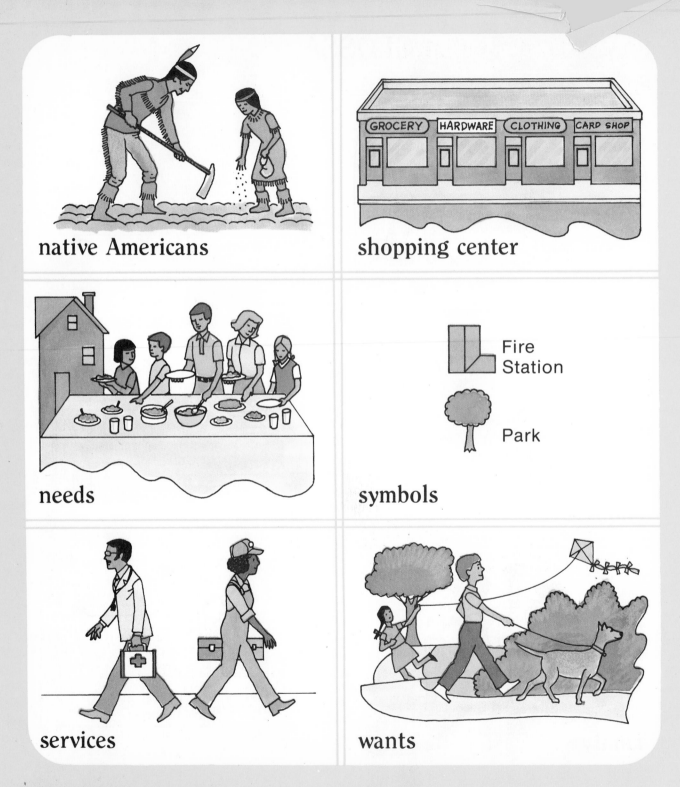

native Americans

shopping center

needs

symbols

Fire Station

Park

services

wants